It's a Cupcake Party!

Text and Photography by

ELISABETH ANTOINE AND ELIZABETH CUNNINGHAM HERRING

SELLERS
PUBLISHING

To my wonderful children, Basile and Eloise,
inspired I am by their endless creativity.
—Elisabeth Antoine

To my husband, Rich, and my two
sweet little cupcakes, Olivia and Isabelle.
—Elizabeth Cunningham Herring

Acknowledgments

We would like to thank our friends and families for their support and for being our cupcake guinea pigs! Tasting the cupcakes was lots of fun, but it may not have been the best thing for our diets.

We would especially like to thank Greg Tobin and Edward Ash-Milby for their advice, and Julie Pauly, Wendy Foster, Kat Lozynsky, and Caroline Cunningham for all their help.

We would also like to thank our agent, Coleen O'Shea, and our publisher, Robin Haywood, for their encouragement and support.

Published by Sellers Publishing, Inc.
Text and photography copyright © 2012 Elisabeth Antoine & Elizabeth Cunningham Herring
All rights reserved.

Sellers Publishing, Inc.
161 John Roberts Road, South Portland, Maine 04106
Visit our Web site: www.sellerspublishing.com
E-mail: rsp@rsvp.com

ISBN 13: 978-1-4162-0688-0
e-ISBN: 978-1-4162-0733-7
Library of Congress Control Number: 2011935331

10 9 8 7 6 5 4 3 2 1

Printed and bound in China.

Contents

Introduction

J ust when you thought it was safe to go back into a bookstore, here comes yet another cupcake book!

Have no fear! There are plenty of great reasons to add *It's a Cupcake Party!* to your cookbook collection (and its companion book *Cupcake Whimsy* by the same authors). This book features a year's worth of season-inspired recipes for scrumptious cupcakes and frostings as well as detailed instructions on how to create a season-themed cupcake topper for each of the 12 months.

Step-by-step instructions accompanied by more than 175 color photos show you how to use fondant — an amazing sugary concoction — to assemble an exquisite cupcake decoration. Composed of sugar, corn syrup or honey, and water, fondant is easy to work *and play* with. Like clay, it can be formed into lots of different shapes. Unlike clay, the end result is edible and tastes delicious!

And don't worry if you've never worked with fondant before. Following this introduction is "Fondant Fundamentals" which will tell you everything you need to know about fondant — from working with it to storing it.

While the fondant toppers are tons of fun to fashion and make a terrific party activity, they can easily be made in advance to use as decorations for birthday or holiday party cupcakes. You can make the toppers 2 days ahead, store them in a cake storage container or on a lightly covered tray, and place them on the cupcakes just before the party starts. Your guests will be wowed by these amazing decorations — so sophisticated no one will believe you made them yourself!

And it's so simple. All you need is a cupcake and frosting, fondant, food coloring, a knife, and a toothpick. With these supplies, you can craft all the creations in this book! No matter what your skill level, you will enjoy making each featured cupcake topper. And by all means feel free to let your imagination take over and create your own masterpiece.

So gather up your supplies, call some friends, and get ready to create these splendid edible works of art. Let the fun begin!

Fondant Fundamentals

A key ingredient in many wedding and other specialty cakes, fondant is a truly amazing substance. It's easy to use, versatile, and can be used to create remarkable sculptures without any kind of special equipment.

Fondant is a very sweet concoction. Though our recipe calls for corn syrup, you can substitute honey for a slightly healthier version. Please keep in mind that the corn syrup called for is the one used in most pecan pie recipes, not the highly processed high-fructose corn syrup that has received a lot of negative attention lately.

That said, we find that commercial fondant is smoother and much easier to use than the homemade variety. In fact, the toppers in this book were all created using commercial fondant. Fondant is available in many different colors. However, we suggest using white fondant and adding food coloring.

Following are some tips to follow when working with fondant:

- After adding food coloring, knead the fondant until the color is evenly blended and you have achieved your desired shade. If you are using gel food coloring (our product of choice), you may want to wear plastic gloves during this process to avoid rainbow-colored hands for the rest of the day. (Once the food coloring is thoroughly mixed with the fondant, you won't have to worry.) It is better to make a little more of each color than you think you'll need, as it may be hard to match the color if you want to use it later.

- As fondant can sometimes stick to surfaces, place parchment paper under the fondant as you work.

- If necessary, you can use a tiny bit of water to "glue" pieces of fondant together. For example, if you need to affix an eye to a figure, and it doesn't seem to be sticking, dip a toothpick in some water and use that to "glue" the eye on.

- When not working with the fondant, place it in a zippered plastic bag or airtight container until you are ready to use it. If stored properly at room temperature, commercial (not homemade) fondant will last for 18 months.

- The fondant toppers can be made up to 2 days ahead. Store them in a cake storage container or on a lightly covered tray at room temperature. (In a more humid climate, you may want to store them in a cool, dry place.)

- Whatever you do, do not store the fondant toppers in the refrigerator or freezer, as this will cause them to get soft and shiny. You should also avoid storing the finished fondant toppers in an airtight container or bag, as this will have a similar effect. It's important that the container not be airtight; you want air to circulate to keep the fondant from drooping.

- For best results, do not place the finished toppers on the cupcakes until you are ready to serve them.

Homemade Fondant
(makes enough for 12 to 18 cupcake toppers)

⅓ cup hot water
⅓ cup light corn syrup (Karo) or honey
5–6 cups confectioners' sugar

Mix together the hot water and corn syrup or honey. Quickly blend in 5 cups confectioners' sugar until smooth. Knead the fondant, adding small amounts of confectioners' sugar until it forms a dough-like ball and doesn't stick to your fingers.

Keep the fondant in an airtight container to avoid drying. If the fondant gets sticky, feel free to knead some more confectioners' sugar into it.

Arctic Antics

Coconut Cupcakes with Vanilla Buttercream Frosting

Baby, it's cold out there! Grab a mug of cocoa and create your own winter wonderland. Don't worry — our dapper little penguin will chase away the winter blahs.

Makes 12 cupcakes.

INGREDIENTS

For the Cupcakes:

1 1/4 cups all-purpose flour
1/2 teaspoon baking soda
1 teaspoon baking powder
Pinch of salt
1/2 cup unsalted butter, softened
3/4 cup sugar
3 large eggs, separated
1 teaspoon vanilla extract
1/2 cup sour cream
3/4 cup sweetened coconut flakes

For the Frosting:

1 cup unsalted butter, softened
1 teaspoon vanilla extract
4 cups confectioners' sugar
2 teaspoons milk
2 cups sweetened coconut flakes

Preheat oven to 350°F (180°C). Place 12 paper baking cups in a muffin pan.

In a medium bowl, mix together flour, baking soda, baking powder, and salt. In a larger bowl, cream the butter and sugar until light and fluffy. Add egg yolks one at a time, mixing well after each addition (reserve the whites in a small bowl). Add the vanilla. Add the flour mix, alternating with the sour cream. Add the coconut and mix well. In a small bowl, beat egg whites until stiff and then fold carefully into cake batter.

Pour the batter into cupcake liners until they are two-thirds full and bake in the center of the oven for 20 minutes or until a wooden toothpick inserted in the center of the cupcake comes out clean. Cool the pan on a rack for 30 minutes before frosting. Store unfrosted cupcakes in an airtight container in the refrigerator for up to 3 days.

For the Frosting:

Cream butter with an electric mixer in a large bowl. Add vanilla and then gradually add sugar, beating well and scraping the sides of the bowl. Add milk and beat until light and fluffy.

Store in the refrigerator until ready to frost the cupcakes. If the frosting gets too hard, let it sit out at room temperature until it's soft enough to spread. The frosting can be stored in an airtight container in the refrigerator for up to 2 days.

You will need:

- Fondant in the following colors: white, black, orange, and color of choice for scarf and hat
- Butter knife
- Small, sharp knife
- Toothpick

1.

Spread frosting evenly over the cupcake.

2.

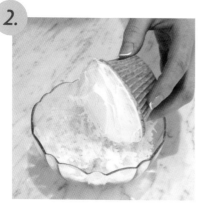

Roll the top of the cupcake in shredded, sweetened coconut.

Take white fondant and make a small ball (the body of the penguin).

Take about the same amount of black fondant and make a ball, then flatten it until it is very thin.

5.

Wrap the black piece around the back of the white fondant ball and pinch the bottom part to form a tail.

6.

With a little black fondant, make 2 cones and flatten them to form flippers. Attach them to each side of the penguin.

7.

Take a small amount of black fondant and roll it into a small ball to form the head. Place it on top of the penguin's body.

8.

Create the eyes using 2 tiny balls of white fondant. Place on the penguin and then add teensy black balls to form the pupils.

9.

With a very small amount of orange fondant, make a triangle to form a beak and place on the penguin.

10.

Make one thin triangle out of orange fondant. Make a slit in the middle with a knife. With a toothpick, add indentations to create the feet. Attach the feet to the bottom of the penguin.

11. Choose whatever color you like to make a scarf and hat. Create a long, thin, flat scarf and make indentations on both ends to form fringe.

12. Carefully wrap the scarf around the penguin's neck.

13.

For the hat, take a small ball of fondant and create a hat shape by shaping the ball around your pinkie. Add indentations on the bottom and a little ball on the top to create a pom-pom.

14.

Place the assembled penguin on top of the cupcake. With leftover fondant, make tiny fish shapes and place in front of penguin.

Bear Hugs and Kisses

Red Velvet Cupcakes with Cream Cheese Frosting

The secret to this cuddly bear's heart is a classic Valentine's Day combination: a scrumptious red velvet cupcake topped with fluffy cream cheese frosting.

Makes 12 cupcakes.

INGREDIENTS

For the Cupcakes:

1 1/4 cups all-purpose flour

1/4 cup unsweetened cocoa powder

1 teaspoon baking soda

Pinch of salt

1/2 cup unsalted butter, softened

1 cup sugar

2 large eggs

1/2 cup sour cream

1/4 cup milk

1 teaspoon vanilla extract

1 teaspoon red food coloring (or more as needed)

For the Frosting:

1 (8-ounce) package cream cheese, softened

1/4 cup unsalted butter, softened

1 1/4 cups confectioners' sugar

Preheat oven to 350°F (180°C). Place 12 paper baking cups in a muffin pan.

In a medium bowl, mix together flour, cocoa powder, baking soda, and salt. In a large bowl, beat butter and sugar together with an electric mixer on medium speed until light and fluffy. Beat in eggs one at a time. Add sour cream, milk, vanilla, and red food coloring, and mix well. Gradually add the flour mixture, using a wooden spoon to mix until just blended. Do not overmix.

Pour the batter into cupcake liners until they are two-thirds full and bake in the center of the oven for 25 minutes or until a wooden toothpick inserted in the center comes out clean. Cool the pan on a wire rack for about 30 minutes before frosting. Store unfrosted cupcakes in an airtight container for up to 3 days.

For the Frosting:

Beat together cream cheese and butter with an electric mixer on medium speed until smooth. Gradually beat in sugar.

Store in the refrigerator until ready to frost the cupcakes. If the frosting gets too hard, let it sit out at room temperature until it's soft enough to spread. The frosting can be stored in an airtight container in the refrigerator for up to 2 days.

- Fondant in the following colors: brown, red, tan, black
- Butter knife

1.

Spread frosting evenly over the cupcake.

2.

With brown fondant, roll a pear shape to form the bear's body.

3.

With the same color fondant, roll 2 small cylinders to form the bear's legs. Flatten and curve the ends as shown.

4.

Place the legs on each side of the body as shown.

5.

Carefully place the body on the cupcake.

6.

With red fondant, form a heart shape. Place the heart against the bear's body as shown.

7.

With brown fondant, roll 2 small cylinders to form the bear's arms.

8.

Place the arms on each side of the body so they hold the heart.

9.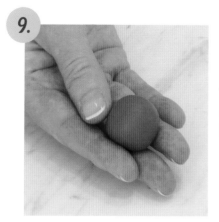

With brown fondant, roll a ball to form the bear's head.

10.

With a small quantity of tan fondant, roll a small ball to form the bear's muzzle. Place it against the head as shown.

11.

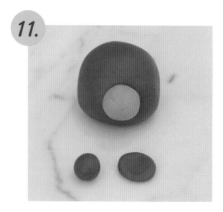

With brown fondant, roll 2 small balls and flatten them to create the bear's ears.

12.

Add a tiny amount of tan fondant to each ear and flatten to form the inner ear. Place the ears on the bear's head.

13.

With a tiny amount of black fondant, roll a little ball to form the nose. Place on the muzzle as shown.

14.

With a tiny amount of black fondant, roll 2 round eyes and affix them to the head. Then place the head on the body as shown.

Lucky Charm

Zucchini Cupcakes with Vanilla Buttercream Frosting

Top of the morning to you! You'll find more than a pot of gold behind this lucky shamrock. There's a tasty zucchini cupcake topped with vanilla buttercream frosting to help you celebrate St. Patrick's Day in green style.

Makes 12 cupcakes.

INGREDIENTS

For the Cupcakes:

1 1/2 cups all-purpose flour
1/2 cup packed light brown sugar
1/2 cup sugar
2 teaspoons baking powder
1 teaspoon cinnamon
Pinch of salt
1/2 cup vegetable oil
1 teaspoon vanilla extract
2 large eggs
1 cup grated zucchini

For the Frosting:

1 cup unsalted butter, softened
1 teaspoon vanilla extract
4 cups confectioners' sugar
2 teaspoons milk

Preheat oven to 350°F (180°C). Place 12 baking cups in muffin pan.

In a medium bowl, mix together flour, sugars, baking powder, cinnamon, and salt. In a separate larger bowl, mix together oil, vanilla, eggs, and zucchini. Gradually add the flour mix to the wet ingredients. Stir well with a wooden spoon until smooth.

Pour the batter into cupcake liners until they are about two-thirds full and bake in the center of the oven for about 35 minutes or until a wooden toothpick inserted in the center of a cupcake comes out clean. Cool on rack for 30 minutes before frosting. Store unfrosted cupcakes in an airtight container for up to 3 days.

For the Frosting:

Cream butter with an electric mixer in a large bowl. Add vanilla and then gradually add sugar, beating well and scraping the sides of the bowl. Add milk and beat until light and fluffy.

Store in the refrigerator until ready to frost the cupcakes. If the frosting gets too hard, let it sit out at room temperature until it's soft enough to spread. The frosting can be stored in an airtight container in the refrigerator for up to 2 days.

1.

Spread frosting evenly over the cupcake.

2.

With black fondant, roll a medium-sized ball.

3.

Use your finger to create a depression in the ball to form a round pot.

4.

Roll some black fondant in a thin sausage shape to create the rim of the pot.

5.

Apply the rim to the pot as shown.

6.

With yellow fondant, roll 10 tiny balls.

7.

Flatten the tiny balls to form gold coins.

8.

Place the coins in the pot, overfilling it slightly as shown.

9.

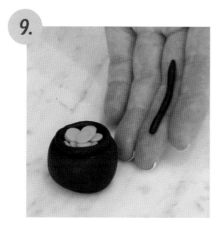

With black fondant, roll another thin sausage shape to form the pot's handle.

10.

Place the handle under the rim and place the pot on the cupcake.

11.

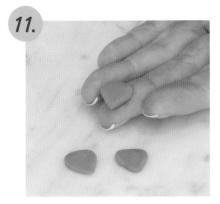

With green fondant, create 3 identical flat triangles.

12.

Attach the triangles together as shown and use a toothpick to create an indentation at the top of each triangle.

13.

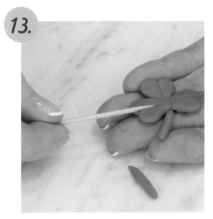

Create a stem by rolling a tiny amount of green fondant. Place the stem under the shamrock. Use a toothpick to create indentations as shown.

14.

Place the shamrock on the cupcake, leaning against the pot.

Out of the Rabbit Hole

Carrot Cupcakes with Cream Cheese Frosting

Spring is in the air! Watch the white rabbit emerge from his enchanted garden to gather some sweet fondant carrots. Shh!

Makes 12 cupcakes.

INGREDIENTS

For the Cupcakes:

1 cup sugar
1 teaspoon cinnamon
½ cup vegetable oil
1 teaspoon vanilla extract
2 large eggs
2 cups peeled and shredded carrots
1 cup all-purpose flour
½ teaspoon baking soda
1 teaspoon baking powder
Pinch of salt

For the Frosting:

1 (8-ounce) package cream cheese, softened
¼ cup unsalted butter, softened
1 ¼ cups confectioners' sugar
Green food coloring

Preheat oven to 350°F (180°C). Place 12 baking cups in muffin pan.

In a large bowl, mix together sugar, cinnamon, oil, vanilla, and eggs. Add the carrots and mix well. In a separate smaller bowl, mix together flour, baking soda, baking powder, and salt. Gradually add the flour mixture to the wet ingredients. Stir with a wooden spoon until well blended.

Pour the batter into cupcake liners until they are about two-thirds full and bake in the center of the oven for about 25 minutes or until a wooden toothpick inserted in the center of a cupcake comes out clean. Cool on rack for 30 minutes before frosting. Store unfrosted cupcakes in an airtight container in the refrigerator for up to 3 days.

For the Frosting:

Beat together cream cheese and butter with an electric mixer on medium speed until smooth. Gradually beat in sugar. Add green food coloring and mix well until blended.

Store in the refrigerator until ready to frost the cupcakes. If the frosting gets too hard, let it sit out at room temperature until it's soft enough to spread. The frosting can be stored in an airtight container in the refrigerator for up to 2 days.

- Fondant in the following colors: white, pink, black, orange, green
- Butter knife
- Toothpick

1.

Spread frosting evenly over the cupcake.

2.

Use white fondant to make a ball to form the bunny's body and a smaller oval ball to form the bunny's head.

3.

Place the oval ball on top of the larger ball.

4.

With a little piece of pink fondant, create a nose and place it on the head.

5.

Take 2 small pieces of white fondant and shape and flatten them to form the bunny's ears.

6.

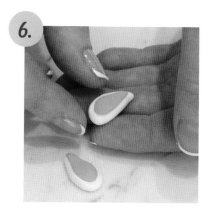

Take 2 tiny pieces of pink fondant and flatten them to form the interior of the bunny's ears. Place them on the inside of the white ears.

7.

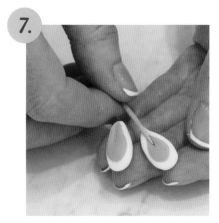

Use a toothpick to make indentations on the base of each ear.

8.

Carefully affix the ears to the bunny's head.

9.

Create the bunny's eyes using black fondant and place them on the bunny's face.

10.

Make 2 small balls with white fondant to form the bunny's feet. Use a toothpick to create indentations for his toes.

11.

Place the bunny on the cupcake and then place the feet in front of the bunny.

12.

Make a carrot shape with orange fondant.

13.

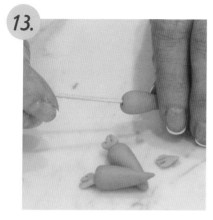

With a little green fondant, make a small flattened triangle and then use a sharp knife to make slits in the wide side to form a leaf. Use a wooden toothpick to make a small hole at the top of the carrot. Insert the leaf in the hole.

14.

Place the carrots around the bunny on top of the cupcake.

Daffodils in Bloom

Yellow Cupcakes with Orange Buttercream Frosting

For any occasion, be it May Day, Mother's Day, or Memorial Day, you can never go wrong with this bright bouquet of sunny daffodil cupcakes!

Makes 12 cupcakes.

INGREDIENTS

For the Cupcakes:

1 1/4 cups all-purpose flour
1/2 teaspoon baking soda
1 teaspoon baking powder
Pinch of salt
1/2 cup unsalted butter, softened
1 cup sugar
3 large eggs, separated
1 teaspoon vanilla extract
1/2 cup sour cream

For the Frosting:

1 cup unsalted butter, softened
4 cups confectioners' sugar
1 teaspoon orange zest
4 tablespoons fresh-squeezed orange juice
2 teaspoons vanilla extract
2 tablespoons light corn syrup

Preheat oven to 350°F (180°C). Place 12 baking cups in muffin pan.

In a medium bowl, mix together flour, baking soda, baking powder, and salt. In a larger bowl, cream butter and sugar together until light and fluffy. Add egg yolks one at a time, reserving the whites in a separate bowl. Mix well after each addition, and then add vanilla. Add the flour mix, alternately with the sour cream. Meanwhile, beat egg whites with an electric mixer on high speed until stiff, and then gently fold into the rest of the batter with a wooden spoon.

Pour the batter into cupcake liners until they are about two-thirds full and bake in the center of the oven for about 20 minutes or until a wooden toothpick inserted in the center of a cupcake comes out clean. Cool on rack for 30 minutes before frosting. Store unfrosted cupcakes in an airtight container in the refrigerator for up to 3 days.

For the Frosting:

Cream butter with an electric mixer on medium speed until smooth. Gradually add sugar, one cup at a time. Add orange zest, orange juice, vanilla, and light corn syrup. Beat until light and fluffy.

Store in the refrigerator until ready to frost the cupcakes. If the frosting gets too hard, let it sit out at room temperature until it's soft enough to spread. The frosting can be stored in an airtight container in the refrigerator for up to 2 days.

1.

Spread frosting evenly over the cupcake.

2.

With green fondant, create a small cylinder about 1 inch in length.

3.

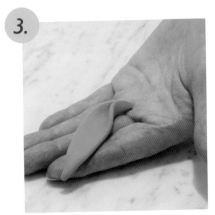

Pinch the cylinder at the end and flatten it to make a leaf shape.

4.

Place the leaf on top of the cupcake.

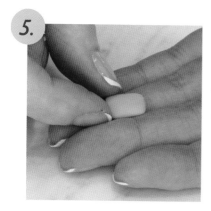

With yellow fondant, create a small flat rectangle.

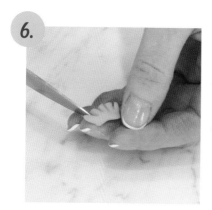

With a small, sharp knife, make slits on the long side of the rectangle.

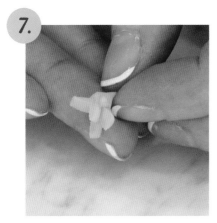

7. Roll the rectangle over itself to create the pistil.

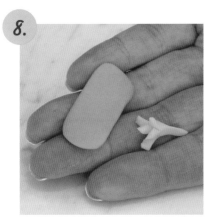

8. With orange fondant, make a flat rectangle.

9.

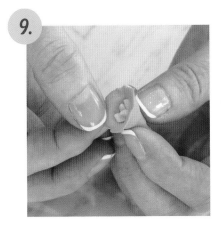

Wrap the yellow pistil in the orange rectangle and crimp the edges to form the corona.

10.

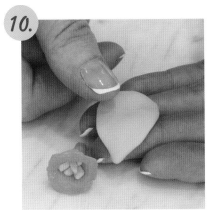

With yellow fondant, create a petal shape.

With a knife, make
indentations in the
petal as shown.

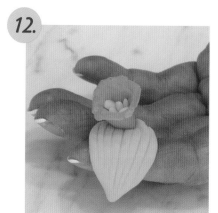

Attach the petal to the base
of the corona.

Make 5 more petals in the same way and overlap them around the corona, then pinch the bottom. For best results, remember to let the flowers dry before positioning them on top of the cupcake.

Just before serving, carefully place the finished flower on top of the cupcake.

Vegetable Delights

Chocolate Cupcakes with Chocolate Frosting

How does your garden grow? Chocolate is the secret of our garden of vegetable delights: carrots, tomatoes, peppers, and radishes never tasted so sweet!

Makes 12 cupcakes.

INGREDIENTS

For the Cupcakes:

4 tablespoons unsalted butter, softened

1 1/2 cups sugar

2 large eggs

1 teaspoon vanilla extract

1 cup all-purpose flour

1/4 teaspoon baking soda

2 teaspoons baking powder

1 cup unsweetened cocoa powder

Pinch of salt

1 cup milk

For the Frosting:

1 cup heavy cream

4 tablespoons unsalted butter

2 tablespoons light corn syrup

10 ounces semisweet chocolate chips

2 cups finely crushed chocolate graham crackers

Preheat oven to 350°F (180°C). Place 12 baking cups in muffin pan.

In a large bowl, combine butter and sugar and mix with a wooden spoon. Add eggs one at a time and blend well. Stir in vanilla. In a separate bowl, combine flour, baking soda, baking powder, cocoa powder, and salt. Gradually add the flour mixture to the larger bowl, alternating with the milk. Stir well until smooth. (Tip: Once the flour mixture has been added to the batter, it's important that you do not overmix it, since doing so can cause the cupcakes to become dense.)

Pour the batter into cupcake liners until they are about two-thirds full and bake in the center of the oven for about 25 minutes or until a wooden toothpick inserted in the center of a cupcake comes out clean. Cool on rack for 30 minutes before frosting. Store unfrosted cupcakes in an airtight container for up to 3 days.

For the Frosting:

Bring cream, butter, and light corn syrup to a simmer in a medium, heavy-bottomed saucepan. Remove from heat and add chocolate chips, mixing until melted and smooth. Whisk occasionally until cool. The mixture will thicken as it cools.

Store in the refrigerator until ready to frost the cupcakes. If the frosting gets too hard, let it sit out at room temperature until it's soft enough to spread. The frosting can be stored in an airtight container in the refrigerator for up to 2 days.

1.

Spread frosting evenly over the cupcake.

2.

Roll the top of the cupcake in finely crushed chocolate graham crackers.

3.

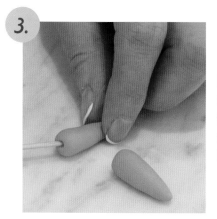

Roll a small ball of orange fondant in your fingers to form a carrot shape. Use a toothpick to make a small hole at the top of the carrot.

4.

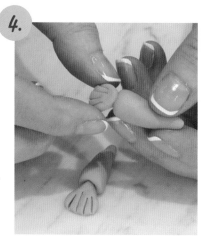

With a little green fondant, make a small flattened triangle and then use a sharp knife to make slits in the wide side to form a leaf. Insert the leaf in the hole at the top of the carrot.

5.

Take a small piece of yellow fondant and form a pepper shape.

6.

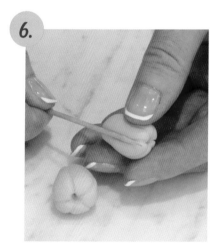

Make indentations on the sides of the pepper with a toothpick and then use the toothpick to make a wide hole at the top of the pepper.

7.

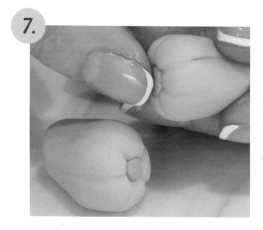

Make a tiny ball of green fondant and gently place it in the hole at the top of the pepper.

8.

For the tomato, use red fondant to form a ball and then flatten it slightly between your fingers.

9.

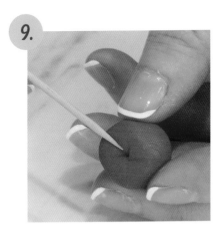

Using a toothpick, make a hole at the top and slight striations emerging from the hole.

10.

Take a tiny ball of green fondant, flatten between your fingers, and use a knife to cut it into a star-shaped leaf. Pinch the center of the star and insert it into the hole at the top of the tomato.

11.

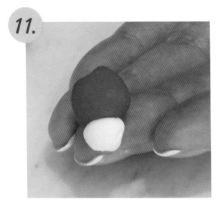

For the radish, bring together a ball of red fondant and a smaller ball of white fondant.

12.

Gently pinch the white part and round the red part to form a radish shape.

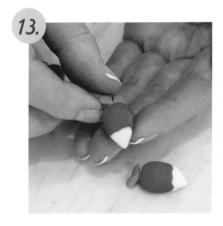

13. Make a hole at the red end of the radish. Use green fondant to make 2 tiny round leaves and insert them in the hole.

14. Arrange the vegetables on top of the cupcake. Feel free to add other vegetables such as mushrooms and stringbeans.

Red, White, and Berry

Confetti Cupcakes with Sour Cream Frosting

Celebrate your 4th of July with a bang! These confetti cupcakes decorated with fondant strawberries and blueberries in a flag configuration are sure to set off fireworks at your next July 4th bbq!

Makes 12 cupcakes.
Note: *To make the flag design pictured here, you will need at least 15 cupcakes, so we suggest you double this recipe.*

INGREDIENTS

For the Cupcakes:

¼ cup milk
¼ cup heavy cream
3 large egg whites
1 teaspoon vanilla extract
1 cup all-purpose flour
Pinch of salt
½ teaspoon baking soda
2 teaspoons baking powder
6 tablespoons unsalted butter, softened
1 cup sugar
2 tablespoons red and blue sprinkles

For the Frosting:

4 tablespoons unsalted butter, softened
½ cup sour cream
1 teaspoon vanilla extract
Pinch of salt
4 cups confectioners' sugar

Preheat oven to 350°F (180°C). Place 12 baking cups in muffin pan.

In a small bowl, mix together milk, heavy cream, egg whites, and vanilla, and set aside. In another bowl, stir together flour, salt, baking soda, and baking powder. In a large bowl, cream butter and sugar. Alternatively add milk mixture and flour mixture to the butter mixture. Do not overmix. Stir in sprinkles.

Spoon the batter evenly into cupcake liners until they are about one-half full and bake in the center of the oven for about 20 minutes or until a wooden toothpick inserted in the center of a cupcake comes out clean. Cool on rack for 30 minutes before frosting. Store unfrosted cupcakes in an airtight container in the refrigerator for up to 3 days.

For the Frosting:

In a medium bowl, beat the butter, sour cream, vanilla, and salt with an electric mixer on medium speed. Gradually add the confectioners' sugar and beat until smooth.

Store in the refrigerator until ready to frost the cupcakes. If the frosting gets too hard, let it sit out at room temperature until it's soft enough to spread. The frosting can be stored in an airtight container in the refrigerator for up to 2 days.

- Fondant in the following colors: dark blue, red, green
- Butter knife
- Toothpick

1. Spread frosting evenly over the cupcake.

2. With dark blue fondant, roll a ball to form a blueberry.

3.

Use a toothpick to make a tiny hole at the top of the blueberry.

4.

Make 4 more blueberries and place on top of one cupcake as shown.

5.

Decorate 3 more cupcakes in the same way.

6.

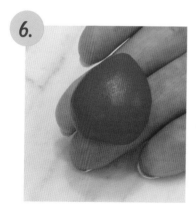

With red fondant, make a small cone shape to form a strawberry.

7.

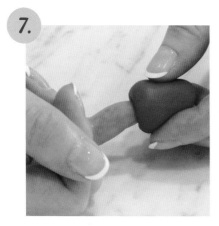

Use your pinkie finger to create a depression at the top of the strawberry.

8.

With a toothpick, make little holes all around the strawberry.

9.

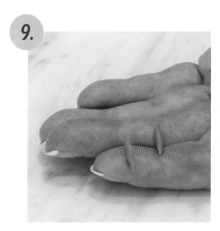

With a tiny amount of green fondant, roll 2 tiny thin cylinders.

10.

Use your finger to flatten each cylinder in the middle.

11.

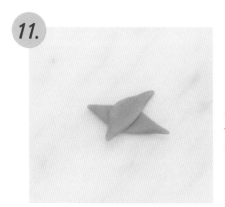

Place the 2 flattened cylinders together so they cross in the middle as shown.

12.

Place the green part in the middle of the depression at the top of the strawberry.

13.

Use a toothpick to create a hole in the middle of the green part. Place the strawberry in the center of a new cupcake.

14.

In order to make the flag pattern shown, decorate 10 more cupcakes in the same manner (with the strawberries) and place them as shown.

Sun, Surf, and Sand

Caramel Cupcakes with Caramel Frosting

Surf's up — time to tackle the waves! You'll have lots of fun in the sun as you feast on these caramel cupcakes topped with caramel frosting and light brown sugar.

Makes 12 cupcakes.

INGREDIENTS

For the Cupcakes:

1 1/4 cups all-purpose flour

1 teaspoon baking powder

1/2 teaspoon baking soda

1/4 teaspoon salt

1/2 cup unsalted butter, softened

1 cup sugar

1/4 cup packed dark brown sugar

3 large eggs

1 teaspoon vanilla extract

1/2 cup buttermilk

For the Frosting:

1/2 cup unsalted butter

1 cup packed dark brown sugar

1/4 cup heavy cream (and more set aside to add later if necessary)

1 teaspoon vanilla extract

1 1/2 cups confectioners' sugar

2 cups light brown sugar

Preheat oven to 350°F (180°C). Place 12 baking cups in muffin pan.

In a medium bowl, mix together flour, baking powder, baking soda, and salt, and set aside. In a large bowl, mix the butter and sugars together and then add eggs one at a time. Add vanilla and buttermilk and blend. Gradually add the flour mixture and mix with a wooden spoon.

Spoon the batter into cupcake liners until they are about two-thirds full and bake in the center of the oven for about 20 minutes or until a wooden toothpick inserted in the center of a cupcake comes out clean. Cool on rack for 30 minutes before frosting.

Store unfrosted cupcakes in an airtight container in the refrigerator for up to 3 days.

For the Frosting:

Melt butter over low flame and add dark brown sugar. Stirring constantly, bring the mixture to a boil. Add heavy cream and vanilla and return to a boil. Remove from heat and let sit at room temperature for 1 hour. Sift in confectioners' sugar and beat with an electric mixer on high until the mixture is creamy. You may need to add a little more cream to achieve the right spreading consistency.

Store in the refrigerator until ready to frost the cupcakes. If the frosting gets too hard, let it sit out at room temperature until it's soft enough to spread. The frosting can be stored in an airtight container in the refrigerator for up to 2 days.

- Fondant in the following colors: blue, green, orange, tan, white
- Butter knife
- Toothpick

Note: *In order for the surfboard to stand up in the cupcake, it must be made the day before and allowed to dry for 24 hours.*

1.

Spread frosting evenly over the cupcake.

2.

Roll the cupcake in light brown sugar so that the frosting is evenly coated.

3.

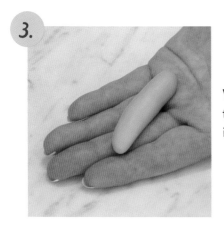

With blue fondant, roll a thick cylinder (about 2½ inches long).

4.

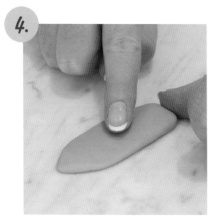

Gently flatten the cylinder with your fingers to form a surfboard shape as shown.

5.

With a small amount of green fondant, roll a long, very thin rope-like shape and place it so that it runs down the center of the board. Press it down.

6.

With orange fondant, make 4 flat petals and apply them to the top of the board as shown.

7.

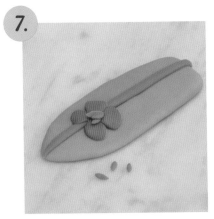

With a tiny amount of green fondant, make 3 tiny pistils and press them in the center of the flower. Set aside for at least 24 hours to allow the surfboard to dry and harden.

8.

Take a small amount of tan and white fondant and knead them together slightly to create a marbling effect.

9.

With a small amount of the marbled fondant, roll 2 very thin elongated cones.

10.

Take 1 of the cones and, starting from the thin end, roll the cone onto itself to form a shell. Use a toothpick to create a big hole at the large end of the shell as shown.

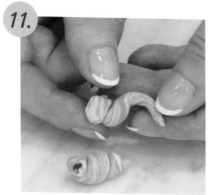

11. Take the other cone and, starting from the large end, roll it into a spiral as shown. Use a toothpick to create a big hole in the large end as shown.

12. With a small amount of marbled fondant, roll a small ball and flatten it. Use a toothpick to create 2 small indentations at the base of the circle.

13.

Use a knife to create indentations in a fan pattern as shown.

14.

Place the hardened surf board standing in the frosting as shown and place the seashells around it.

A is for Apple

Cinnamon Applesauce Cupcakes with Vanilla Buttercream Frosting

You'll be the apple of your teacher's eye when you present this delicious cinnamon applesauce cupcake topped with vanilla buttercream frosting. It's a great way to start the school year before hitting the books!

Makes 12 cupcakes.

INGREDIENTS

For the Cupcakes:

½ cup unsalted butter, softened

¾ cup packed brown sugar

1 cup unsweetened applesauce

1 large egg

1½ cups all-purpose flour

1 teaspoon baking soda

1 teaspoon cinnamon

¼ teaspoon nutmeg

Pinch of ground cloves

½ teaspoon salt

For the Frosting:

1 cup unsalted butter, softened

1 teaspoon vanilla extract

4 cups confectioners' sugar

2 teaspoons milk

Preheat oven to 375°F (190°C). Place 12 baking cups in muffin pan.

In a large bowl, mix together butter and brown sugar. Blend in applesauce and egg. In a separate bowl, mix together flour, baking soda, cinnamon, nutmeg, cloves, and salt. Gradually add the flour mixture to the batter and blend well.

Spoon the batter into cupcake liners until they are about two-thirds full and bake in the center of the oven for about 30 minutes or until a wooden toothpick inserted in the center of a cupcake comes out clean. Cool on rack for 30 minutes before frosting. Store unfrosted cupcakes in an airtight container in the refrigerator for up to 3 days.

For the Frosting:

Cream butter with an electric mixer in a large bowl. Add vanilla and then gradually add sugar, beating well and scraping the sides of the bowl. Add milk and beat until light and fluffy.

Store in the refrigerator until ready to frost the cupcakes. If the frosting gets too hard, let it sit out at room temperature until it's soft enough to spread. The frosting can be stored in an airtight container in the refrigerator for up to 2 days.

- Fondant in the following colors: white, yellow, red, brown, green
- Butter knife
- Small, sharp knife
- Toothpick

Spread frosting evenly over the cupcake.

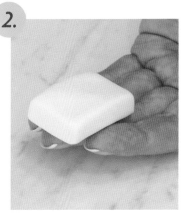

With white fondant, make a flat rectangle to create the pages of a book. (The example shown is about 1 inch wide, 1½ inches long, and ¼ inch deep.)

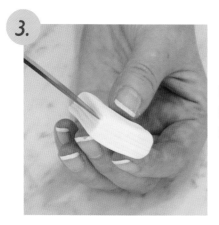

Use a knife to create indentations to imitate pages as shown.

With yellow fondant, make a thin flat rectangle to form the book's cover. (The example shown is about 1¾ inches wide by 3 inches long.)

5.

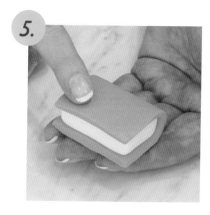

Wrap the cover around the pages as shown and press lightly to adhere.

6.

Place the book in the center of the cupcake.

7.

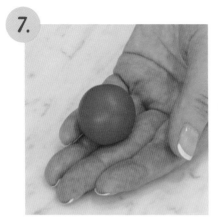

With red fondant, roll a ball.

8.

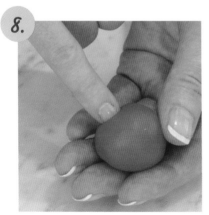

Use your pinkie finger to create a depression in the ball to form the top of an apple, and shape the rest of the ball to resemble an apple as shown.

9.

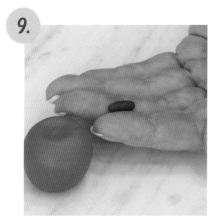

With brown fondant, roll a tiny cylinder to create the stem.

10.

Use a toothpick to make a hole in the middle of the top of the apple and insert the stem.

With green fondant, create a flat leaf shape.

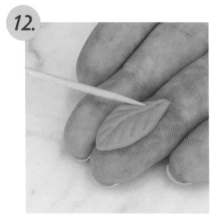

Use a toothpick to make indentations to form the leaf's veins.

13.

Place the leaf in the depression at the top of the apple next to the stem.

14.

Place the apple on top of the book.

Monster Mash
Devil's Food Cupcakes with Chocolate Ganache Frosting

Gripping a bone, our fiendishly funny green-spotted monster struggles to unearth himself from a ganache-frosted devil's food cupcake — what a yummy way to end a monster mash bash!

Makes 18 cupcakes.

INGREDIENTS

For the Cupcakes:

3 ounces unsweetened chocolate

$\frac{1}{2}$ cup unsalted butter

2 cups packed dark brown sugar

2 large eggs

2 teaspoons vanilla extract

2 cups all-purpose flour

2 teaspoons baking soda

Pinch of salt

$\frac{1}{2}$ cup buttermilk

1 cup boiling water

For the Frosting:

2 cups bittersweet chocolate chips

1 cup heavy cream

Preheat oven to 350°F (180°C). Place 18 baking cups in 2 muffin pans.

Melt chocolate and butter together in a double boiler. In a large bowl, stir together the melted chocolate mixture with sugar. Add the eggs and vanilla and mix until well blended. In a small bowl, mix the flour, baking soda, and salt. Add about half the flour mixture to the chocolate batter, then add the buttermilk, and then the rest of the flour mixture. Stir gently with a wooden spoon until well blended. Add the boiling water and stir.

Pour the batter into cupcake liners until they are about two-thirds full and bake in the center of the oven for about 20 minutes or until a wooden toothpick inserted in the center of a cupcake comes out clean. Cool on rack for 30 minutes before frosting. Store unfrosted cupcakes in an airtight container in the refrigerator for up to 3 days.

For the Frosting:

Place the chocolate chips in a large bowl. In a small saucepan, bring the cream almost to a boil. Pour the hot cream over the chocolate and stir until smooth. The frosting will thicken as it cools.

Store in the refrigerator until ready to frost the cupcakes. If the frosting gets too hard, let it sit out at room temperature until it's soft enough to spread. The frosting can be stored in an airtight container in the refrigerator for up to 2 days.

You will need:

- Fondant in the following colors: green, orange, black, lime green, light pink, white
- Butter knife
- Small, sharp knife
- Toothpick

1.

Spread frosting evenly over the cupcake.

2.

Using the green fondant, make a ball.

3.

Using a small, sharp knife, create an opening for the mouth.

4.

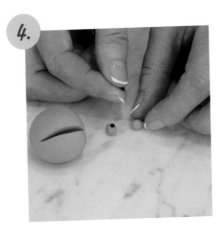

Use orange and black fondant to form the eyes.

5.

Attach the eyes to the head and press the head firmly onto the top of the cupcake.

6.

With lime green fondant, create 2 small horns.

7.

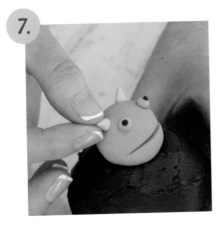

Attach the horns to the monster's head.

8.

Make tiny spots out of lime green fondant and affix around the monster's head.

9.

Use light pink fondant to make a tongue and use a knife to make a groove in the center. Carefully place the tongue in the monster's mouth.

10.

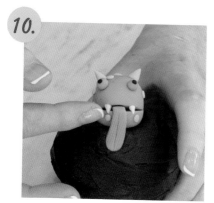

Make 2 tiny pointed teeth out of white fondant and place them on either side of the tongue in the monster's mouth.

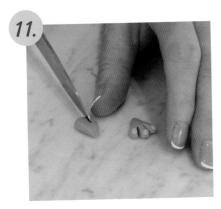

11.

For the monster's hands, make 2 triangles using dark green fondant. With a small, sharp knife, make 2 cuts in each to form fingers, and add lime green nails.

12.

Place the hands in the frosting as shown.

13.

With white fondant, make a bone shape. Use a toothpick to create the indentations on both sides.

14.

Carefully place the bone beside one of the monster's hands.

Wild Turkeys

Pumpkin Cupcakes with Cream Cheese Frosting

Seems like this trio of wild turkeys may have wandered into the wrong place at the wrong time! Trot away, wild turkeys, before someone decides to gobble, gobble, gobble you up!

Makes 12 cupcakes.

INGREDIENTS

For the Cupcakes:

1 cup all-purpose flour
1 cup sugar
1 teaspoon cinnamon
1/4 teaspoon nutmeg
1/4 teaspoon ground cloves
1 teaspoon baking powder
1/2 teaspoon baking soda
Pinch of salt
1 cup solid canned pumpkin (not pumpkin filling)
2 large eggs
1/4 cup plus 2 tablespoons vegetable oil

For the Frosting:

1 (8-ounce) package cream cheese, softened
1/4 cup unsalted butter, softened
1 1/4 cups confectioners' sugar

Preheat oven to 350°F (180°C). Place 12 baking cups in muffin pan.

In a large bowl, mix together flour, sugar, cinnamon, nutmeg, cloves, baking powder, baking soda, and salt. In a medium bowl, mix together pumpkin, eggs, and oil. Add the pumpkin mixture to the flour mixture and stir with a wooden spoon. Do not overmix.

Pour the batter into cupcake liners until they are about two-thirds full and bake in the center of the oven for about 25 minutes or until a wooden toothpick inserted in the center of a cupcake comes out clean. Cool on rack for 30 minutes before frosting. Store unfrosted cupcakes in an airtight container in the refrigerator for up to 3 days.

For the Frosting:

Beat together cream cheese and butter with an electric mixer on medium speed. Gradually beat in sugar until smooth.

Store in the refrigerator until ready to frost the cupcakes. If the frosting gets too hard, let it sit out at room temperature until it's soft enough to spread. The frosting can be stored in an airtight container in the refrigerator for up to 2 days.

- Fondant in the following colors: brown, red, orange, yellow, white, black
- Butter knife
- Toothpick

1.

Spread frosting evenly over the cupcake.

2.

With brown fondant, roll a pear shape to form the turkey's body.

3.

With a smaller amount of brown fondant (about ⅓ the amount used for the body), roll a ball, flatten it, and cut it into a fan shape with a small, sharp knife to form the tail.

4.

Roll a small amount of red fondant into a long, thin sausage shape, and press it along the curved side of the tail as shown.

5.

Roll a small amount of orange fondant in the same way, and press it beneath the red fondant as shown.

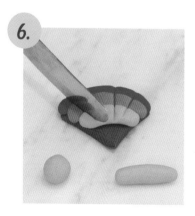

6.

Roll a small amount of yellow fondant, and press it under the orange fondant. Use a knife to make indentations to form the feathers as shown.

7.

Attach the tail to the body by pressing the large part of the body into the base of the fan.

8.

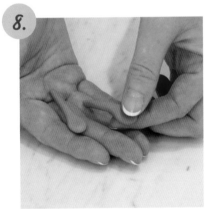

With orange fondant, roll 2 long logs to form the legs. With your finger, flatten the ends of each leg to form the turkey's feet.

9.

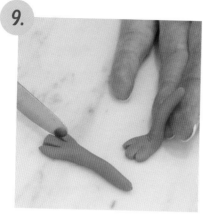

With a knife, cut 2 slits in each foot to create the toes. Angle the feet as shown.

10.

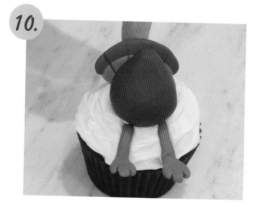

Position the legs on the cupcake and carefully place the body on top as shown.

11.

With brown fondant, roll a small ball to form the head and place it on top of the body.

12.

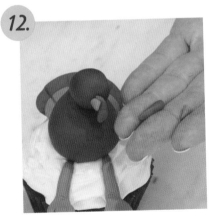

With a little orange fondant, create the beak and place it on the turkey's face. With a small amount of red fondant, form the turkey's wattle and press it on the side of the beak.

13.

With white fondant, create 2 eyeballs and affix them above the beak. Use a tiny amount of black fondant to create pupils and place them on the eyeballs as shown.

14.

With brown fondant, create 2 flat tear-shaped wings. Use a toothpick to create indentations for the feathers and affix the wings on each side of the turkey as shown.

Le Snowman

Chocolate Brownie Cupcakes with Mint Mascarpone Frosting

This fashionable French snowman will help you celebrate your holidays in elegant French style. Sporting a beret, he even comes with a baguette and a bottle of Bordeaux. Bon appétit!

Makes 12 cupcakes.

INGREDIENTS

For the Cupcakes:

4 ounces unsweetened chocolate
1 cup unsalted butter
1 cup all-purpose flour
1¾ cups packed light brown sugar
Pinch of salt
4 large eggs
1 teaspoon vanilla extract

For the Frosting:

1¼ cups confectioners' sugar
6 tablespoons unsalted butter, softened
4 ounces cold mascarpone
¼ teaspoon peppermint extract

Preheat oven to 325°F (170°C). Place 12 baking cups in muffin pan.

In a medium saucepan over low heat, melt together chocolate and butter and stir until smooth. Set aside to cool. In a large bowl, mix together flour, sugar, and salt. Add eggs one at a time and blend well. Stir in vanilla. Add the chocolate mixture to the flour mix and stir well.

Pour the batter into cupcake liners until they are about three-fourths full and bake in the center of the oven for about 25 minutes or until the tops of the cupcakes spring back when lightly pressed. Do not overbake. Cool on rack for 30 minutes before frosting. Store unfrosted cupcakes in an airtight container in the refrigerator for up to 3 days.

For the Frosting:

In a medium bowl, beat the sugar and butter with an electric mixer on medium speed until light and fluffy. Add the mascarpone and peppermint extract and stir until smooth.

Store in the refrigerator until ready to frost the cupcakes. If the frosting gets too hard, let it sit out at room temperature until it's soft enough to spread. The frosting can be stored in an airtight container in the refrigerator for up to 2 days.

You will need:

- Fondant in the following colors: white, tan, dark brown, black, orange, burgundy
- Butter knife
- Toothpick

1.

Spread frosting evenly over the cupcake.

2.

With white fondant, roll an elongated ball to form the snowman's body.

3. With tan fondant, roll a small baguette shape and, with a toothpick, add scoring to the top of the baguette as shown.

4. Press the baguette against the side of the snowman's body as shown.

5.

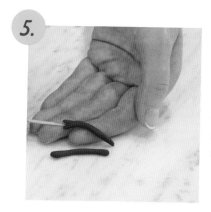

Roll a small quantity of dark brown fondant to create 2 long, thin, branch-like arms. With a toothpick, divide the ends to create the snowman's hands.

6.

Make a hole on each side of the body and insert each arm. Bend the arms in the middle to create an elbow as shown. Bend one arm so that it appears to hold the baguette.

7.

With black fondant, form 3 little buttons and place on the front of the body. Carefully place the body on top of the cupcake.

8.

With white fondant, roll a small ball to form the snowman's head.

9.

With black fondant, roll a small ball and press it in the middle with your index finger to form a beret. Place it on the snowman's head. Add a tiny pom-pom to the top.

10.

With black fondant, make 2 small eyes and place on the snowman's face.

11.

With a little orange fondant, roll a carrot shape. With a toothpick, make a small hole on the snowman's face and insert the carrot as shown.

12.

Roll a tiny amount of black fondant in the shape of a mustache and place below the carrot nose.

13. Place the head on top of the body.

14. With some burgundy fondant, roll a little wine bottle. Add a tiny white label as shown and place the bottle next to the snowman.

Table of Equivalents

Some of the conversions in these lists have been slightly rounded for measuring convenience.

VOLUME:

U.S.	metric
¼ teaspoon	1.25 milliliters
½ teaspoon	2.5 milliliters
¾ teaspoon	3.75 milliliters
1 teaspoon	5 milliliters
1 tablespoon (3 teaspoons)	15 milliliters
2 tablespoons	30 milliliters
3 tablespoons	45 milliliters
1 fluid ounce (2 tablespoons)	30 milliliters
¼ cup (4 tablespoons)	60 milliliters
⅓ cup	80 milliliters
½ cup	120 milliliters
⅔ cup	160 milliliters
1 cup	240 milliliters
2 cups (1 pint)	480 milliliters
4 cups (1 quart or 32 ounces)	960 milliliters
1 gallon (4 quarts)	3.8 liters

OVEN TEMPERATURE:

fahrenheit	celsius
250	120
275	140
300	150
325	160
350	180
375	190
400	200
425	220
450	230
475	240
500	260

WEIGHT:

U.S.	metric
1 ounce (by weight)	28 grams
1 pound	448 grams
2.2 pounds	1 kilogram

LENGTH:

U.S.	metric
⅛ inch	3 millimeters
¼ inch	6 millimeters
½ inch	12 millimeters
1 inch	2.5 centimeters